critters by the sea

CRABS ON THE BEACH

JONATHAN POTTER

PowerKiDS press.
New York

Published in 2018 by The Rosen Publishing Group, Inc.
29 East 21st Street, New York, NY 10010

First Edition

Editor: Melissa Raé Shofner
Book Design: Tanya Dellaccio

Photo Credits: Cover Universal Images Group/Getty Images; pp. 3–24 (background image) Kemal Mardin/Shutterstock.com; p. 4 mastersky/Shutterstock.com; p. 5 duangnapa_b/Shutterstock.com; p. 7 (top) Krista Kennell/Shutterstock.com; p. 7 (middle) Claude Huot/Shutterstock.com; p. 7 (bottom) Cuson/Shutterstock.com; p. 8 Hong Vo/Shutterstock.com; p. 9 trubavin/Shutterstock.com; p. 11 (top) Volvox volvox/Oxford Scientific/Getty Images; p. 11 (bottom) Jeff Rotman/Photolibrary/Getty Images; p. 13 Radu Razvan/Shutterstock.com; p. 15 Stephen Belcher/Minden Pictures/Getty Images; p. 16 Joanna Zopoth-Lipiejko/Shutterstock.com; p. 17 (top) David Williams/BIA/Minden Pictures/Getty Images; p. 17 (bottom) Jean-Edouard Rozey/Shutterstock.com; p. 19 (top) Peter M. Fisher/Corbis/Getty Images; p. 19 (bottom) Stuart Monk/Shutterstock.com; p. 20 jiangdi/Shutterstock.com; p. 21 Mark Wilson/Getty Images News/Getty Images; p. 22 GUDKOV ANDREY/Shutterstock.com.

Cataloging-in-Publication Data

Names: Potter, Jonathan.
Title: Crabs on the beach / Jonathan Potter.
Description: New York : PowerKids Press, 2018. | Series: Critters by the sea | Includes index.
Identifiers: LCCN ISBN 9781538325834 (pbk.) | ISBN 9781538325131 (library bound) | ISBN 9781538325841 (6 pack)
Subjects: LCSH: Crabs–Juvenile literature.
Classification: LCC QL444.M33 P68 2018 | DDC 595.3'86-dc23

Manufactured in the United States of America

CPSIA Compliance Information: Batch #BW18PK: For Further Information contact Rosen Publishing, New York, New York at 1-800-237-9932

CONTENTS

CRAZY CRABS!

Crabs are really cool creatures. They breathe like fish but can also live on land. Most can't run forward, so many run sideways. Most crabs live in the salty ocean. Over time, many crabs **adapted** to living in freshwater, such as lakes and rivers. Still others have adapted to living on land.

Crabs, like lobsters and shrimp, belong to a class of animals called **crustaceans**. Crustaceans don't have bones. Instead, they have an exoskeleton, which is a hard outer covering that **protects** their soft body.

SEA CREATURE FEATURE

The smallest species, or kind, of crab is the pea crab. These little crabs only grow up to 0.75 inch (1.9 cm) across. Some of them live inside oysters!

If you visit a beach, keep an eye out for crabs. Be careful if you pick one up—it might pinch you!

CRABS OF ALL KINDS

Crabs come in many sizes and colors. They can be found around the world. Different kinds of crabs live in different places. For example, mangrove land crabs live under mangrove trees on the beaches along the Caribbean Sea.

Dungeness crabs can grow to be more than 10 inches (25.4 cm) wide. They're found from California to Alaska. Sally Lightfoot crabs come in many colors, from spotted brown to bright red, blue, and yellow. They're common on the Galápagos Islands.

SEA CREATURE FEATURE

There are more than 9,500 species of crabs!

DUNGENESS CRAB

SALLY LIGHTFOOT CRAB

FIDDLER CRAB

There are more than 90 kinds of fiddler crabs. Male fiddler crabs sometimes look like they're playing the fiddle when they move their claws.

SO MANY LEGS!

Crabs have 10 jointed legs. "Jointed" means they're able to bend. Crabs use eight legs for walking. In some species, the back pair of legs is used for swimming or digging. A crab's two front legs have powerful claws. These claws are used for catching food and scaring predators.

Like fish, crabs use **gills** to breathe. Crabs can breathe out of water, too. Land crabs have special ways to keep their gills from drying out. Their gills must be wet to work!

SEA CREATURE FEATURE

Blue crabs use their wide back legs to paddle through the water. They're great swimmers!

Crabs' knees bend sideways. This makes it easier for them to move sideways rather than forward. They move faster this way, too!

GIANTS OF JAPAN

Japanese spider crabs are the biggest crabs in the world. Their legs are really long! They can grow to be up to 13 feet (4 m) long from the tip of one claw to the other. Their bodies are only a small part of this, measuring 15 inches (38.1 cm) or less.

Japanese spider crabs eat the bodies of dead sea animals that have fallen to the ocean floor. They also eat shellfish. These crabs don't weigh very much, even though they look huge!

SEA CREATURE FEATURE

Crabzilla is one of the largest living Japanese spider crabs. His front legs are each more than 5 feet (1.5 m) long! He's appeared on display in aquariums around the world.

Japanese spider crabs live deep in the Pacific Ocean near Japan. They're often found more than 1,000 feet (304.8 m) down.

ON THE HUNT

Crabs aren't picky eaters. They'll often eat whatever lands on the ocean floor. This includes dead fish and plants. Some species of crabs have strong claws they use to open the shells of oysters and other crustaceans—including other crabs! Some crabs have thin claws with sharp, pointed edges, perfect for catching fish.

Freshwater crabs that live in rivers and lakes eat water plants, fish eggs, and frogs. Crabs that live on land may eat bugs and worms.

SEA CREATURE FEATURE

Most crabs hunt at night. During the day, they rest and hide from birds and other hungry predators.

Many types of crabs will eat whatever they can catch. They use their claws to break up their meal before digging in.

GROWING AND MOLTING

Crabs have a lot of babies! Some female crabs lay millions of eggs at a time. Female crabs carry their eggs under their stomach until the eggs are ready to **hatch**.

Once hatched, it may take up to a month for baby crabs to grow shells. As they grow, crabs molt. This means they grow a larger shell under their old one. When their old shell breaks, they climb out. It takes a few hours for their new shell to harden. Young crabs molt more often than older crabs.

SEA CREATURE FEATURE

Baby crabs are called larvae. Crab larvae go through several stages as they grow.

On Christmas Island, Australia, millions of red crabs move from the forest to the coast each fall. During this time, the crabs mate and the females place their eggs into the ocean.

HUNGRY PREDATORS

Crabs make tasty meals for many animals. They're eaten by octopuses, sea gulls, and even other crabs! Crab larvae are easy **prey** for fish. Crabs are in the most danger when they're molting and their new shells are still soft.

Some crabs use **camouflage** to help them hide from predators. Harlequin crabs have bright spots that make them look like their surroundings. Other crabs run away instead of hiding. Ghost crabs run so fast they seem to disappear.

SEA CREATURE FEATURE

Crabs have tiny eyes on the ends of eyestalks to help them watch for danger. They can turn their eyestalks to see in all directions. Crabs can also pull their eyestalks inside their shells.

Sometimes crabs use their strong claws to fight back against predators. If they lose a claw or a leg while fighting, it will grow back over time.

FISHING FOR CRABS

Fishing for crabs is a popular activity around the world. It's fun and fairly easy. There are a number of ways to catch crabs. Today, most people use crab pots, which are special cage-like traps filled with fish or other meat. They come in many different shapes and sizes.

Soft-shell crabs are crabs caught just as they finish molting. Their new shells are still soft at this time. When eating soft-shell crabs, people eat the whole crab!

SEA CREATURE FEATURE

People who fish for crabs are called crabbers. Crabbers need to be careful to avoid crabs' strong, sharp claws.

You can also catch crabs by tying a piece of bait to a fishing line and dropping it into the water. When you feel a crab grab on, bring up the line and scoop up the crab with a net!

CRAB POTS

A TASTY CATCH

Blue crabs live along the Atlantic coast from Nova Scotia to Argentina. The males have bright blue legs and claws. The females have bright orange tips on their claws that make it look as if they have painted nails. While all crabs can run sideways, blue crabs also swim sideways!

Steamed blue crabs are a favorite dish for people living near the Atlantic Ocean. This is because blue crabs have very sweet meat. Many people along the Atlantic coast used to earn a living by catching crabs.

SEA CREATURE FEATURE

Until recently, nearly half the blue crabs caught in the United States came from the Chesapeake Bay area, along the coast of Maryland and Virginia.

The Chesapeake Bay area is known for its blue crabs. In recent years, pollution and overfishing have reduced the number of blue crabs here.

CARING FOR CRABS

Overfishing is a problem for crabs in many places. People have taken steps to control crab fishing to make sure populations remain healthy. Pollution is also a big issue. It creates problems for crabs as well as for people and many other animals that depend on crabs for food.

To find out more about crabs, visit your local zoo or aquarium. Your local librarian will also be able to help you find more information about these cool sea creatures!

GLOSSARY

adapt: To change in order to live better in a certain environment.

camouflage: Colors or shapes on animals that allow them to blend in with their surroundings.

crustacean: An animal with a hard shell, jointed limbs, feelers, and no backbone.

eyestalks: Body parts that hold up some animals' eyes.

fiddle: A stringed musical instrument.

gill: The body part that animals such as fish use to breathe in water.

hatch: To break open or come out of.

mate: To come together to make babies.

pinch: To press hard between teeth, claws, or fingers.

prey: An animal hunted by other animals for food.

protect: To keep safe.

INDEX

WEBSITES

Due to the changing nature of Internet links, PowerKids Press has developed an online list of websites related to the subject of this book. This site is updated regularly. Please use this link to access the list:
www.powerkidslinks.com/seac/crab